I LIVE AN ARMY ✦ LIFE, ✦

I am an Army Wife

By

Valerie Senetha Miles

PublishAmerica
Baltimore

First printing

At the specific preference of the author, PublishAmerica allowed this work to remain exactly as the author intended, verbatim, without editorial input.

ISBN: 1-4137-9141-7
PUBLISHED BY PUBLISHAMERICA, LLLP
www.publishamerica.com
Baltimore

Printed in the United States of America

DEDICATION

This book is dedicated to *my son*, never forget your past, for it teaches you how to make your future so much better, and to *my husband Reu*, for being such a supportive man.

ACKNOWLEDGEMENTS

To my Lord and Savior Jesus Christ for whom I would not have been blessed with this opportunity had it not been for him.

To my friends and family for always supporting me through the good times and the bad. I would try to name them all but I might leave someone out and then they would get me so I won't name anyone.

And last but certainly not least to PublishAmerica Publishing Company for making a dream come true.

CHAPTER ONE

The freeways and the runways are my life. Matt, my husband, came home from work and said, "Honey, we're moving to Alabama."

"Alabama," I said. I spent the whole day daydreaming about the move. I wonder what Alabama is like.

Is it safe? Will I be able to find a job? We had just been married a few months ago. How would I handle being so far from home? I could only cook chicken and pork chops. You know, that simple stuff. Nothing fancy.

And to top things off Matt was a firm believer in an old fashioned wife. You know, be a good cook, a good housewife, smart etc. What in the hell have I gone and done. Oh well, you've got to start somewhere.

I had just graduated from college and had never been away from home. I had taken a job at the mall right after we got married. He went on to Kentucky first to get settled in and I stayed back. It was hard being apart right after marriage, but we managed. Probably because we knew it was only for a short time.

We were living in Fort Knox, Kentucky at the time. Matt was attending the Officers Maintenance Course. I did not work when I was there. So I was pretty darn bored most of the time.

We lived in an efficiency apartment so that should tell you there was not much to do.

There was a maid that came by to do the cleaning. We went out most of the time for dinner, that was about it. About a month before we were to move, Matt buys me a car. I was so excited. My first car.

I didn't have a car in high school. I always drove my mom's car or my sister or aunt or someone in my family. I never had my own car until now. I couldn't believe it. I didn't even think about driving from Kentucky to North Carolina for vacation, and then from North Carolina to Alabama for the move.

Oh my God. Just the thought of it made me nauseous. I hated driving except for in my hometown. But outside of Tarboro! No way. Cars zooming by you like bats out of hell. Cutting you off, riding your bumper! Just makes you want to scream.

The day we left I was so nervous. I had the windows rolled up and the radio off. I don't even think I was breathing half the time. I was so scared, driving across states by myself.

I didn't know where I was going. When we stopped for gas, Matt came over to my car and laughed. He said, "Val, you are going to suffocate if you don't roll these windows down and relax." Relax, is he crazy! Now Matt was driving a Volkswagen Scirroco sports car.

And I was driving a little Mazda 323. He already thinks he is Richard Petty. Now picture him driving down the freeway 75 mph in a sports car and me scared out of my mind trying to follow him in my little Mazda 323. It felt like my poor engine was going to explode. I prayed the entire way there.

But mostly I could have zapped some of those darn drivers right off the rode. They will pass you driving 100 miles an hour and then get in front of you and slow down. Or they won't be paying any attention to what they are doing and they will pull right out in front of you, and act like they did nothing. Those are the times that I wish I was bewitch so that I could twitch my nose and the foolish driving fools would be right back on the road where they were before they pulled out in front of you.

Imagine them. They would be going crazy wondering how in the hell that happened. And I would be driving along laughing my head off and giving three snaps to Elizabeth Montgomery! When we reached North Carolina, I wanted to jump out of the car and never get into another one again. As our vacation ended I was dreading the drive to Fort Rucker, Alabama.

The day we left, my nerves were shot. Here we go again. Another drive behind Richard "Matt" Petty. And when we got to Atlanta I thought I was going to have a nervous breakdown. Oh my God!

If you have ever driven in Atlanta then you know exactly what I am talking about. Where did all those people come from? And is the speed limit there 145 mph and nobody bothered to tell me! Now I know how it feels to desperately need a drink. And I don't mean soda.

And the funny thing is, I am not even a frequent drinker of alcoholic beverages. But let me tell you. I could have used a sip of Jack Bean, or Jim Daniels or vice versa. You know what I mean. I told you I wasn't a frequent drinker.

When we reached the post at Fort Rucker, Alabama we went to Matt's new unit. One of the soldiers there offered to show us to the guesthouse. We were following him when all of a sudden we were stopped by the military police. They went to Matt's car and told him that he didn't come to a complete stop at the intersection we just passed. Ok, you have got to be kidding me.

The speed limits on base are like 10 mph. Of course you know we were driving much slower because we had been driving all day and all night and they said we didn't stop at an intersection. Matt explained to them that he did make a complete stop. He said, "Guys, I am new to the post. I have been driving for fourteen straight hours."

They had about four MP cars surrounding us like we had robbed a bank or something. I was so tired that when they came back to my car and asked for my ID Card, I said, "look, I am tired, we have been driving all day and all night, just give us the ticket and let us go find a bed… And finally after about fifteen or twenty minutes they let us go. What a way to be introduced to a new duty station. Made me want to leave already and we had just got there.

My, My, My I am not too sure about this military life! We then went on to the guesthouse and got registered in. Boy was I tired, and ready to get a long shower and pass out. I was so tired of living out of a suitcase and very ready to get into my own house.

The next morning Matt and I went to the post housing office to sign up for housing. This was a new experience for me. Signing up for housing. Ok, here we go. There were several names ahead of us so we were very surprised when we were called four days later to sign for a house.

We had heard that a normal wait for military housing was at least 6 months if you're lucky. I was thrilled. Finally, I can pack those suitcases away. Thank God! Now for the good part, or so I thought.

Furniture. We had none. So when we moved into our house we slept on sleeping bags and we had one TV and our clothes. You see we got married straight out of college. I was still living with my mother and his first tour was in Korea so we had no need to buy furniture.

The TV we had was the very same one that Matt bought me in college. When transportation came to bring Matt's household goods, which he had from his Korea tour, all he had was his clothes, a TV, and a stereo system. So we were starting from scratch. So when the weekend came, we went out to shop for furniture.

I was so excited. My first shopping experience for furniture. Well that is, for my own house. But what was I thinking. Matt was pretty tight with the almighty dollar. He was not going to buy something too expensive.

And that he did not. We were on a budget. Budget? New house. First house. New furniture. Budget furniture? Somehow this did not go together to me.

I will never forget it. It was a wood set with plaid pillows. Yuck! You know the kind that if you ran into it and stomped your toe or something it would feel like you broke it! But that is what we got.

But at least we had furniture. Those sleeping bags just were not cutting it. Finally, a house with furniture and no suitcase living. At least for the time being. So we finally settled in and Matt started his new job.

And I started out on what turned out to be a nightmare. Job-hunting. What a headache. Matt was a Lieutenant and we were just starting our lives together, so I wanted to work so I could carry out one of my life-long passions.

CHAPTER TWO

Shopping! This was a plague to Matt. He believed that if it wasn't ragged or near destruction it was salvageable and did not need to be replaced, and that shopping was not a necessary function unless an emergency arose, meaning groceries or something like that. That was the first shock of being a newlywed. No spur of the moment shopping!

Oh my goodness! That was not in the marriage vows. Was there some kind of secret marriage vow book that banished shopping and I didn't know about it? Well I see right now this is going to be a problem! Anyway, I never thought job hunting could be so depressing.

After a while, I found a job. It was at Wendy's in Dale City, Alabama. Yes I started out as a salad bar girl. Ok what's wrong with this picture. Graduate from college, get married move around and land a job at Wendy's.

That must have also been in that hidden marriage vow book. Well I worked there for a while and then I got a job in the Base Exchange. Or the PX is what the soldiers call it. My job at the PX was part time so I continued to work at Wendy's and the PX for a while. Ok, I really didn't like this.

Working two jobs and can't shop. What a bummer. I never stopped my search for a job in my field of studies which was business. After a while, I found a job in a little town about fifteen miles from post called Ozark, Alabama. It was a fertilizer company called Frit Industries.

So I resigned from Wendy's and the PX and started working there. The people were wonderful at Frit Industries and soon became like a family to me. I really liked this job. I was a sales secretary there and I handled administrative duties for the field salesmen and also made up samples for them to distribute to their customers. It was fun. I enjoyed my work there.

We had been in Alabama for a while when in October of 1989 I became pregnant. Oh my God! Pregnant, away from home, no family just my new husband. This is not looking good! What do I do? Will it hurt? Geese, Louise, whose bright idea was this.

Having a baby. Was that in the plan? What plan? Ok I am freaking out now. Calm down Val. You can do this. Could somebody please slap those voices that are saying this stupid stuff! Well the bigger I got the more miserable it was.

Thank God for the sofa in the ladies restroom at work. It saved me so many times. And thank goodness for Coca Cola and Saltine crackers. I lived off those things while I was pregnant. Well I was overdue and it was driving me crazy.

This baby needs to come out already. On July 4th the base always has a big 4th of July bash. Well Matt and I went over to some friends house for the celebration. Matt and some of the other guys walked down the street to see some of the fireworks going on. I was back at the house eating when all of a sudden I felt a pain.

And then another pain. Oh my God. Somebody was doing a number on me. But at the time I was eating Barbecue spare ribs, corn on the cob, collard greens and cornbread. Well maybe I could stand a pain or two to finish up a southern meal like this one.

A couple of the wives got a little nervous and ran down the street to get Matt. They told him that I was in labor. He comes running back to the house where I was asking me if I was in labor. I told him yes. So after I finished my spare ribs, we went to the hospital.

I had not dilated enough centimeters so they told me to walk the halls at the hospital for a while. That sucked because every time I had a contraction I had to stop. Finally they gave me a bed and funny thing about that is they hook you up to a machine that lets you know when you are going to have a contraction. So every time I got ready to have a contraction Matt told me. After about the third time I told him to stop telling me, duh! I know already! I'm having the pains buddy!

Seventeen hours went by and finally the baby was coming. But of course he got a little nosey and would not hold his head down. The doctor kept trying to push his head down so that he could come out but he was a stubborn little man already! Then my temperature spiked a little too high and the doctors were a little concerned so they did an emergency caesarean and out came an eight-pound boy. Matthew Jr. A handful I must say.

When Christmas came around Matt was put in charge of a program called Operation Santa Claus. This is a program on military installations where the soldier's collect and repair donated toys for families in need of assistance. Matt was excited about the program. He really threw himself into this project. Matt loves kids.

If it were up to him we would have had three or four. He even went out to the surrounding cities promoting this program. He even went out and bought some new toys for the program. The wives in our unit were also involved in this program. We collected stuffed animals and dolls.

We had meetings and we even took bags full home and washed them, combed hair, and made clothes for the dolls. We were preparing them for distribution. The project went very well.

Saturday was my day at the commissary. That is the military grocery store. So I'd grab my coupons and calculator and off I'd go. Yes I had to go to the store with a calculator and coupons because Matt was a tightwad. Remember, "the budget." I hated to go to the commissary during those days. When we were just starting out we were on a tight budget.

So when I went to the commissary it was such a depressing task. I only got what was on my list. Yes! Absolutely no splurging in that house. Meanwhile, things were heating up in the Persian Gulf. The guys were on alert and everyone was a little scared.

There was a possibility that they might have to go there. God, this was frightening. Everyone was on pins and needles praying that his or her husband or wife would not have to go. But of course that traumatic time approached when everyone was preparing to go. Matthew Jr. was only three months old when that day came.

The military buses were lined up waiting to load the soldiers on and drive them away. Newspaper reporters, TV reporters were all there at the departure ceremony taping the teary goodbyes. Uncertainty was pouring as the fate of these husbands and wives lie in limbo. The field was filled with rucksacks, duffle bags, weapons, etc. This was a day I would not want to relive.

Spouses were teary eyed, children were crying, the day was just a gloomy one. Getting shipped off to possible war was scary for everyone. Especially for a couple of newlyweds like Matt and I. What in the world would we do without each other? We just had a new baby.

I had no family near me. No one to help. Was I ready for this? Could I handle this? So much unsurity. Saying goodbye to your loved one going off to war was something I didn't know if I could deal with.

We were so young. What if something happened? What would I do? Pray a lot. The next six months were pure hell. There were wives left back that were pregnant, some didn't have transportation, some had no license.

So much was going on. And before the soldiers left for Saudi

Arabia they had to make out wills, and power of attorneys to leave with their spouses. Believe it or not some of these wives actually let their husbands leave without doing these things. Which left them in up the creek situations.

Some were not listed on their husband's checking accounts, some didn't know what bills needed to be paid or how much to pay on them. They gave checks to their spouses over in Saudi and were not keeping up with what checks either were writing, or by the time he or she found out what checks the other one wrote, it was too late and checks were already bouncing all over town. It was just a mess. Ladies, Ladies, Ladies! Never, never put yourself in a position like this.

Always get involved in the finances of your relationship. Always inform yourself of bills, insurances, and accounts. I mean, not just for things like deployment, but any situation could occur. Accidents or anything. It is just very important that you know these things.

There were family support groups and there was a rear detachment group left back that aided spouses. They mowed the lawns for spouses, changed oil in automobiles, check cars, and helped out as much as they could. The family support groups were helpful to those wives who needed assistance. They assisted spouses in reading LES's (leave and earning statements) and kept them informed as to what their spouses in Saudi Arabia were doing. And they tried to provide us with as much information as possible.

I was so very happy when they set up phone lines and I received my first call from Matt. I could tell that he was concerned about the baby; after all, he was only three months old when he left. I also knew that he had faith in me and he knew that our son would be well taken care of. Before Matt went to Saudi Arabia he made cassette tapes talking to Matthew Jr., and everyday for six months I played those tapes to Matthew Jr. so he would know his dad.

I can't say that it wasn't difficult taking care of Matt all by myself but it definitely was an experience. After all he was my first and he was a good little boy. He was a happy baby not too fussy and ate like a champ. He didn't mess around with that baby food stuff. He wasn't taking too kindly to that. He was grabbing for mash potatoes, macaroni and cheese, that kind of food.

You should have seen some of the faces he made when I tried to feed him baby food from a jar. He wasn't having it! After a few months all hell broke loose. Some of the wives and husbands were not receiving calls or letters from their spouses in the Persian Gulf. They would call and ask me if I had talked to Matt.

Matt called me as often as he could and I was content. I wrote him diligently every day. So many wives were not receiving letters or calls. As the months went by, wives got buck wild. I don't know if it was restlessness or what, but all I know is they started hanging out and it was getting back to the spouses over in Saudi Arabia.

It was a mess. I mean these soldiers were over there putting their lives on the line and they were probably more worried about what he or she was hearing about his or her spouse than about their lives. It was unbelievable. Meanwhile, I bought an answering machine and spent a lot of time, Matt Jr. and I, with the ladies at work. They were all so very nice and Ms. Nancy could cook!

When I moved to Alabama I met two military wives, Patricia and Voncille. Pat worked at the main exchange and Von lived near Pat. We would go out to the track and walk and then hit the gym to work out. Von and I would go shopping and to dinner. She was always trying to keep my chin up during this whole Saudi Arabia ordeal.

One day when I came home from work and turned on the news I saw that firing had begun in the Persian Gulf. My heart sunk. I was breathless. My phone rang and for a split second I was terrified to answer it. I didn't know what to think. Is this bad news? Should I answer this?

I finally got the nerve to answer and it was Matt's Commander's wife. She wanted to know if I had seen the news. I told her yes, and I think she was in just as bad of shape as I was. My phone was ringing off the hook. I was a mess.

I could not answer it for a while. I tried to get myself together but I just couldn't. This is tearing my nerves to pieces. I am too young for this kind of stress I kept telling myself. What would I do if something happened to Matt?

How could I handle it? Could I handle it? Or would I fall to pieces. I couldn't do that, I had Matt Jr. What would I tell him if something happened to his dad? Raise a son on my own.

All these things were running through my head. There I go again wishing for a stiff drink. You know, I am so glad that I don't drink or I probably would have been a stone alcoholic by age 25! Hah!

My mother called to see if I was okay. She was very supportive during the entire time Matt was deployed. My mother, my salvation. I don't know what I would do without her. I think everyone in my family called me almost everyday after the fighting started. I was really glad. I needed the support.

These were very trying times. We were hearing on the news about reserve barracks being hit and all sorts of scary things. All we could do is pray that this was nowhere near your spouse. I was so nervous that my boss had a radio at work so I wouldn't miss any special news reports. Matt also had a sister deployed with a reserve unit in Saudi Arabia, so I was equally afraid for her as well.

She found Matt shortly after she got over there so I think they kept in touch as much as possible. I know that had to be hard for him knowing that his sister was over there and in just as much danger as he was. She had two children at home with her mother so I know that was a lot of stress on her. Matt's family were very close so they were all pitching in moral support for him and his sister. His family kept in close contact with me also.

They tried to keep me from worrying and I tried to keep them from worrying. But I don't think it was working for either one of us. We couldn't help but be worried. I must say that this was the worst six months of my entire life. Waiting and not knowing is so stressful.

And after all that torture of waiting, the time drew near when our loved ones would be returning home hopefully safe and sound. About three weeks before they were scheduled to return home my phone rang. It was Matt's mother. Matt's brother William, had been killed in a pedestrian accident. I was speechless.

William was special. He was known all over his hometown. People loved him. And he looked like Smokey Robinson! He was nice to everyone.

He was especially nice to me the first time he met me. He was the kind of person that didn't have much, but would offer you his last, not thinking about what he would not have but that he was helping someone else. How could I tell Matt this? God I hated this. This is definitely not the homecoming I anticipated.

Why did this have to happen? I called the Red Cross and then they called Matt's parents to get all the information in order to notify Matt. But before they could notify Matt, he called me. Oh my! Do I tell him… don't I tell him?

How could I act as if nothing was wrong? I couldn't pull it off. Just tell him. So unfortunately I had to be the bearer of bad news. I didn't know how Matt would take this because he was very close to his brother.

He seemed okay when I told him but deep down I knew he was very hurt. We were miles away from each other but I could feel it. I could feel the pain and I knew that it must be difficult for him to hold it in. They notified his sister at the same time. I don't know if they got to see each other when they told them.

Matthew Jr. and I were sitting at the airport waiting for Matt to come in. I saw people getting off the plane but no Matt. "Gosh," I said, " Is he on the plane." By then everyone was off the plane and we were still waiting, when all of a sudden I saw this BDU Army green uniform getting off the plane. Finally, it was him.

I was thrilled. Of course the first thing he did when he saw us was grab Matt Jr. He was so very happy to see him. I really think that Matt Jr. recognized his voice from the cassette tapes. He responded very well to him.

Especially with him being gone for six months. Matt was small. He looked like he had loss weight. But I guess they didn't have time to think about eating over there. Well, after our happy homecoming, sadness broke in and we were on our way to Windsor, North Carolina for the funeral.

These were sad times but we survived and went on with our lives. The funeral was extremely sad because as I said Matt's family was very close. And no matter where one of them were they all always kept in touch. However, after the funeral we had to head back to Alabama. The fields were being prepared for the rest of the troops to return.

With flags and banners everywhere the area was filling up with families awaiting the soldiers return from Saudi Arabia. Everyone was so excited and happy. When the troops landed and marched on the field the families couldn't wait to rush out on the field and greet them. As the homecoming reached an end the problems started to evolve and all hell broke loose once again. People were filing for divorces, legal separations, you name it.

So many things had gone on during the Gulf War. Spouses were returning home to find affairs had taken place, spouses had not carried themselves respectably. It was amazing. I'm sure any military installation that was involved in the Gulf War had their own horror stories. Matt, Matt Jr. and I were just enjoying his return.

We had six months of catching up to do. Stories to tell, things that happened. All about my job. Things that Matt Jr. had done that he had missed. He could not believe how big Matt Jr. had gotten.

He wanted to spend as much time as he could with Matt Jr. Matt came home from work and said, "Val, guess what?" "They gave me a school date for the advanced course at Fort Leonard Wood, Missouri." So we have to move. Boy, oh boy! Not again.

And to Missouri. Oh God. So the movers came over to pack our household goods. Then we started to clean our house for the inspection. Yes, if you're living in military housing, your house has to be cleaned and inspected before you can clear the post.

Your military spouse has to go through in processing when coming to a new duty station and they have to go through out-processing when they leave a duty station. Anyway, the housing inspectors are very picky. So we cleaned everything that they had on the checklist and when the inspector came out we were packed and ready to give him the keys and get on the road. He comes in, checks the house and tells us we can't pass because the refrigerator was on with ice trays in it. Tell me this isn't picky.

You have got to be kidding me right? When I cleaned the refrigerator I plugged it back in and put the ice trays back in the freezer part. Isn't that what most people would do? Where is that stiff drink again! I think this is how I got addicted to sodas.

Every time something crazy happened to me I would grab a Pepsi. Go figure! Now tell me this, couldn't he had just told us to unplug the refrigerator and take the ice trays out an then let us go? No, instead he told us we had to call for another appointment. I was so mad.

Ok this is a hoax right? And we are on America's Funniest Home Videos? Nope. Guess again. So after we unplugged the refrigerator and took out the trays, we called to set up another appointment, and luckily we got one for the same day at three o'clock.

CHAPTER THREE

Then we were on our way. Missouri. Fort Leonard Wood, Missouri or as many soldiers called it Fort Lost in the Woods of Misery. I totally agree. Especially with the misery part. When we got to Missouri, we signed for housing about two days later.

The wait wasn't so long because who wants to go to Missouri. Nobody in his or her right mind. Matt had a brother who was a military reserve 1LT stationed there also. We signed for housing and then set up an appointment for transportation to bring our household goods out.

They were very small quarters and most of our things had to be put in storage. Since the tour was so short most of the wives did not work. There was nothing close to Fort Leonard Wood Missouri other than Wal-mart. I signed up for aerobics classes and started making a few crafts. That was about the just of my days there.

Boring was the word for this duty station. At least for me it was. I could not get out of there fast enough. Matt started classes and the stress kicked in. The advanced course was very demanding.

It required conviction so when the guys weren't in class they were at home either doing assignments, exercising for PT test or typing projects on the computer. Of course since I was not working that meant no leisurely shopping for me! That really sucked! Was it possible to do an I Dream of Jeanie blink and be out of there! Talk about on a scale of one to ten duty station this one ranked at about a –3!

I was so ready to leave that place I think I would have packed the household goods truck myself. And believe it or not there were some soldiers that had Fort Leonard Wood as their tour duty station. That meant they were there for 3 or 4 years. No way Hose'. That is one tour that Matt would have had to do by himself.

I would have kicked and screamed like a baby if I had to stay there for 3 or 4 years. They call it the "Show Me" state. Yeah! Show me how to get the hell out of there! Goodbye! Our next duty station move was Hawaii. No you didn't misunderstand.

Yes I said Hawaii. Aloha Ohe'. Don't you just love all this moving. What a life! My middle name should be guesthouse, suitcase, rest stop, Hotel.

That's the story of my life. And the story for most military spouses. They have this saying that goes "If the Army wanted you to have a wife they would have issued you one." Well, I think a wife is the first thing the army should issue out! I believe in that old saying, "behind every good man there is a good woman."

Military spouses are dependent warriors. While Matt goes out every day to train to defend his country, I'm training to keep our family together, strong and happy. In actuality, your spouse is on call to work 24 hours in the army, and so are you. I get up in the morning when Matt leaves for PT. I make sure he has everything; his uniform, breakfast and lunch.

Then I get Matt Jr. ready for preschool while getting myself ready for work. I drop Matt Jr. off to school then I go to work. On my lunch break I run errands. I pick up dry cleaning, toothpaste, deodorant, shoe polish, write out bills, and mail them off all in an hour, and then it's back to work. I am at the office meeting deadlines, going through my in-box, answering phones.

A 4:30 pm I rush to pick up Matt Jr. from school. Then I go home, take out dinner to defrost, change my clothes and Matt Jr.'s, start a load of laundry, cook dinner, then give Matt Jr. a bath. When Matt gets home I have to wash his PT uniform, serve dinner, then get Matt Jr. ready for bed. Then I make lunch for Matt for the next day, do the dishes, take a shower and pass out. And the next morning when the alarm clock goes off I feel like picking Matt up and throwing him at the clock! What a life!

CHAPTER FOUR

Hawaii, what a beautiful state. It is always so pretty over there. Even when it rains it only last about 2 minutes and then the sun is right back out. It's not too hot and it's not too cold, it's like Goldilocks found porridge, it's always just right! After arriving in Hawaii late that night our sponsors met us at the airport, then drove us to the hotel.

I was beat. Matt was assigned to the 84th Engineer Battalion on Schofield Barracks. The next day when Matt went to work he put our names on the housing list which was ridiculously long he said. Now we were only qualified for a two bedroom house because we only had one child. That's how it works.

So we had to find off-post housing until on-post housing became available. We wanted a three bedroom house, but we could only receive a three bedroom house if one became in excess and then we had to be able to accept it as soon as it was offered. Well if you were in a fixed lease then that was impossible. I hated packing and moving and I didn't want to move into a house and stay for 18 months, then pack up to move on post. So we decided to take a house off post.

When our household goods arrived I was worried about what to expect. God I hoped all our things were there and not broken, or busted up. When they started bringing our things in I was marking them off my list. One of our speakers to our stereo system was missing. Now why would someone take one speaker!

My cordless phone was missing. God knows what else. By the time I went through all the boxes I was disgusted. After several moves you start to go crazy! You stand there and watch them pack every single thing and label each box.

You start keeping all of the original boxes and your receipts when you purchase things. This is how picky you start to get. By the time you go through every box, you have a claim form as long as your arm. Then when you turn it in, by the time they depreciate everything on the list you get about a third of what you actually need to replace and repair your valuables. Matt would always say we have so many phone numbers because of moving so much that by the time he learns it, then it's time to move again and he has to learn another one.

After a couple of days Matt and I usually take a tour of post trying to find those important places like the commissary, PX, hospital, dry cleaners, credit union, housing, civilian personnel, daycare, gas station and the furniture store. (the last one is for me of course! Smile). We wanted to familiarize ourselves with post. Schofield is not a big post. It didn't take too long for me to find everything. I always say, an important item to a military spouse is the phone book because, believe it or not, Matt calls me for every number he needs.

The phone book and the military directory; two key items to keep at arms reach. After being here for about three weeks I started looking for a daycare for Matt Jr. This is the most difficult task for military families. You're never anywhere for more than three or four years, if that long. Normally it's three years then you're off to somewhere else.

Unless you ask for an extension. Otherwise you're moving on! It is so hard on your children. They're moved over and over again. The difficulty also depends on their ages.

If the children are older they make friends and then soon after have to leave them, move and make new friends all over again.

The transition can be a very difficult one. Even for younger kids like Matt Jr., transition can have a negative affect. If they are in daycare or preschool he or she gets to know the teachers, and they develop a relationship. The children become comfortable there and then before you know it it's time to go.

It is so hard. And it's even harder trying to find a good daycare or childcare provider. I am very particular about daycares since most of the time I am new to the area and don't know anyone. So it's hard and you have to take chances. And if they don't work out then you have to end up moving them again.

And you really hate putting your child through this. They have daycare facilities on military post too. These are usually the first choice for most military families if they have openings. But most of the time their waiting lists are just as bad as the housing waiting list. And on most of the military installations the amount you pay is based on your income, which I personally feel is unfair because each individual child is receiving the same care and instruction that is offered in that classroom but parents are paying based on their salary and not on a base fee.

So you may have some parents paying $500 a month and some parents paying $200 a month at the same facility. I am certain though that facility directors will give you some kind of reason for this. You might not agree with the reason but I'm sure they'll give you one! After I placed Matt Jr. in daycare, I started looking for a job. Remember, I had a passion for shopping and I couldn't engage in my passion if I was not gainfully employed.

Job-hunting for a military spouse is one of the most traumatic experiences that could ever happen in a person's life. So you start out pounding the pavement into the world of work. You start out with two strikes against you. One, you're a woman and no matter what people say, it is still a major factor. Two, you're a military dependent, meaning you're here for a couple of years and then you're moving on.

With this in mind, job hunting can be so frustrating. That is why you have a lot of military spouses that are homemakers because sometimes it is not even worth the hassle. So I prepare my resume, put my suit on and I'm off. As I enter into office after office applying for positions in my field, filling out applications, going through interviews, wondering what the interviewer is thinking and knowing that you are more than qualified for the position. Then you always hear that same old thing, "Well, we have a few more interviews lined up and then we will make our decision.

We will be in touch with you." You know those lines by heart. Yeah, don't call us, we'll call you. Those famous words. So I kept pounding the pavement until my feet ached and I'm so tired I just can't think straight, so I call it a day and I head home to start dinner.

Another disappointing day of job hunting. Don't you just hate it! Why must we endure such trauma! Can't we start getting paid for this housewife stuff! I mean cooking and cleaning and laundry and that God-awful dishwashing!

You should get paid at least $100 for washing dishes. I hate washing dishes. And using a dishwasher. What's the difference? I mean most people rinse the dishes before they put them in the dishwasher so you might as well wash those suckers and keep going!

Then you have the cleaning. Scrubbing toilets and showers and floors. Yuck! And next you have cooking, which is so unfair. Because when you cook you're going to taste test while you're cooking then most of the time it is after 5pm when you get home from work so it is around 6:30 or 7pm before you eat dinner. That spells a recipe for weight gain!

Which puts a monkey wrench in trying to keep that girlish figure you had when you were in college and dating your now husband. That is so funny! Every wife out there is on the floor laughing hysterically because she knows I am so right about that. And you try to eat healthy but if you're married to a country boy like Matthew healthy goes on the back burner. He was a fried chicken, mash potatoes and gravy, and cornbread kinda guy.

Oh and lets not forget the apple pie with vanilla bean ice cream on top for dessert. And ladies is there some kind of marital ice cream clause in the wedding vows that say ice cream is like toilet paper. There must always be some in the house. If I did not have any ice cream in the house I think Matthew would go in to convulsions. Ice Cream was always at the top of the grocery list.

Oh and that chocolate topping that hardens when you pour it on. That must be one of those things that are the small fine print in the marriage vows, love, honor, cherish and provide ice cream treats on a moments notice!

When Matthew gets home from work he says to me, "Val, I don't know about this job."

By then I was so frustrated with job hunting that I say, "Well at least you have a job."

He looks at me and says, "So I guess your day didn't go so well."

When I finished cooking dinner and got Matthew ready for bed and tucked in I pulled out the newspaper and combed those help wanted ads religiously. I was looking for something in my field and a good location. Oh goodness, how I dread this! It is really difficult now trying to get in the Civil Service system due to the hiring freeze and you have to go through so much. First you have to take a Civil Service examination if you want to apply for any clerical position.

Then you have to score a certain grade in order to apply for certain permanent positions. If you pass the exam but score below a certain grade you can only apply for temporary positions. Keep in mind, this was back in 1994. What a headache. There are other positions you can apply for. These are called Non-appropriated fund vacancies.

These don't require testing. With the Civil Service positions once you take the exam and pass with the required score your name is put on a list and when positions become available names are selected from the list. In the meantime you can apply for positions that are posted at the civilian personnel office. You'd think on a military installation a military spouse should have no problem acquiring positions on the post. But you will find that at a lot of the duty stations you go to some of the people that live in the communities as permanent residents hold a lot of the positions on post.

Being that these people will be here forever they will keep these positions, leaving less positions for the spouses to obtain. This is frustrating for any military spouse. So we continue to pound that pavement and sometimes have to settle for those low entry-level positions because you have no other choice if you want to work. And by the time you're there long enough for a promotion its time for you and your family to PCS. So at your next duty station you're right back where you started.

I'll never forget the first coffee I attended. I had no idea what a coffee was. After all I was twenty-two years old. Fresh out of college. Had absolutely no education of the military.

So when Matt started explaining things to me I was stunned at first. I was never a socializer so this was going to take some work. I had never done any entertaining. I thought to myself, God I feel like I need some type of instruction manual on how to be a military spouse. Hell, at the time I didn't even wear many dresses.

The military was very new to me. But Matt was wonderful. He gave me as much guidance as he possible could. And he informed me of everything going on. When I met the Colonel's wife in Alabama, she told me when the coffees were held, how often and where they were held.

She told me that you could either have it at your house or at a restaurant. The wives signed up for which month they wanted to host a coffee. During the meetings, the Colonel's wife usually discusses the business. She gives us information that she obtains from meetings which she attends. The Commander's wives in turn take this information and pass it along to members of their company level family support group.

These activities are voluntary, although initially you feel that if you don't participate it will have some effect on your husband' career. And although it is said over and over again that the wife's participation holds no negative influence on your husband's career, you wonder and you always have that thought in the back of your head. The family support groups are held at company levels for each individual company. The group is to support the soldiers and their families. These groups are mostly active during deployment.

Although there is support all the time. The support group is also for single soldiers. I think that a lot of the single soldiers don't think that it's for them, but it is. It is just as much for them as it is for soldiers with families. I know if I was a single soldier I would definitely want people that I could mingle with, go to for help or information or even just to get involved in some of the activities that are provided.

When Matt and I moved to Hawaii and he took command of a company, we organized an Adopt a Single Soldier Program, where families in our company would adopt a soldier or more than one and invite him or her over for the holidays, or Sunday dinner or even just so they could get away from the barracks for a while. Matt and I had fun doing that. This Christmas we really enjoyed having several of the single soldiers over. It was nice having all the families over enjoying the holiday together because Matt, Matt Jr. and I were not able to spend the holidays with our families all the time since we were always so far away from them. We tried to make the holidays enjoyable for all of our guests.

We had karaoke, food, drinks, the works. Matt, being the comedian that he was, always provided some type of entertainment for everyone. His singing, well that's a story in itself and he would always sing songs and if he didn't know the words he would make up some! Hilarious he was! Sometimes the words he made up for the song would have you laughing so hard your side would hurt.

Now picture a group of soldiers singing karaoke and not knowing the words to the songs. Funny thought huh! At least it took your mind off not being able to be with your family during the holidays. You weren't so lonely and missing everybody. My family would not even consider flying so them visiting was out of the question.

Matt's family didn't do a lot of traveling either. I am really ready to move on now. You move around so much that after you have been somewhere for a while you get restless and ready to leave. The only thing about that is where you will go from here. Sometimes you end up in some of the crappiest places.

Posts that are miles from civilization, no malls for thirty miles. You have to drive miles into the nearest town to find a job. The post is boring. You hate it so much you start x-ing off the days on the calendar as to your departure date. You can't wait to leave there when suddenly you realize- Oh no!

What if the next duty station sucks like the last one did? Oh my God. It saddens my heart to see the stress and frustration in Matt's eyes as he goes through another day at work. Is it fair for one man to be held accountable for over 200 adults? Is it fair that one man's career lies in the wings because of other people's actions?

Of course afterwards you can think of several ways you could have handled the situation but at the time of the incident you do what you feel is best at that time. Matt's a really strong person and he takes it all in stride. I don't know how he does it. He always says, "Val, if deep in my heart I feel I've done the right thing then I'm okay with myself." But I tell him everyone's heart isn't as big as yours. People don't care.

Yes, that is exactly how I see it. And with today's cutbacks by the president, everyone is a little uneasy. Now soldiers might have to make a career change before they plan to. Soldier's lives are in turmoil because of this uncertainty. No one knows what lies ahead.

Well, at least the Army is offering an early out program with some pay. The soldier can choose to get out early and request a bonus or pay incentives offered to soldiers who choose to voluntarily get out because of the cutbacks. The Army is a job and an adventure. You never know what's going to happen from one day to the next. I must say this is not a job that I could deal with.

The stress would drive me bananas. I respect soldiers of all branches of the service because they have to be very flexible, interchangeable people. They have to be caring and strong because you're never anywhere for long. And they must also instill a lot of courage and independence into their family members because they have to be apart from their families so very often. That's a real part of our lives.

A part that you don't like but you get used to. All military wives go through those army woes. You know the postal service probably knows you on a first name basis. The phone company loves you. When Matthew took command of a company I literally had to call his office in order to touch base with him because most of the time when he gets home it's so late that he just eats dinner, checks in on our son, Matthew, and he showers and goes to bed.

I might get a "Hi honey" somewhere in between all that. Then they have their field problems where they'll be gone for a week or two. My mother teases me a lot. She says don't you get lonely with the field problems, short-term deployments, school assignments and TDY trips. I told her that I'm used to it now so when I get that 24-hour notice I just go with it.

When we do decide to settle down, I'll probably start having nightmares about moving. And then I'll wake up and say, "Oh, thank goodness I was dreaming." There is one good thing about moving though. If you get a duty station that you just hate then you know you look forward to those three years ending so you can pack up and move. Military people have a tremendous amount of pictures.

Ask any military family and they'll probably tell you that they have tons of photo albums. Pictures of all the places they've been. And pictures that we take of each other. So you can tell your children, "Yes, this is your dad."

Yes, he lives with us. Sometimes it's funny. Sometimes it's depressing. All the time it's real. I'm really proud of Matt because deep down I know he hates being away from his family, as I'm sure most soldiers do. And I know he hates moving all the time and missing some of Matthew's activities but yet he knows this comes with the job.

I think that our family has adjusted to military life. I can't say I like all of it, but I've adjusted. If there is such a thing as adjusting. Do you ever? I am definitely ready to get back to the mainland.

Hawaii is nice, but I would rather be just a little closer to my mother. And I'm not too keen on flying. I'm just praying that our next duty station is a really nice place with good neighborhoods, good schools, nice malls and last, but not least, good job opportunity. Please don't let us get stuck in some little hick town where everyone there has been there forever and will be there until they die and have the entire town's jobs already. I dread that happening to us.

I keep thinking that with all the post closings that duty stations are going to be limited as well as on-post housing. And I'm just sorry but after I've lived in a house for a year and a half there's no way I'm going to pack up all my things and move again, then a year and a half later move again to PCS. No way. Sometimes I wish that duty stations were permanent, that you could choose which duty station you wanted to go to and just stay there. And only if you wanted a new job then be moved.

Yeah, wishful thinking, I know. Fat chance, I know. Well it doesn't hurt to dream. A duty station on the beach, a good paying job when you get there. Wow, wouldn't it be nice though?

Couldn't you just imagine it? Ok, Ok I went off on the deep in there for a minute. I'm back to reality now. Like I said before, Fat chance right! But I must say that the military has given me a look at a life that otherwise I would not have known.

I mean unless you are pretty wealthy who could do this much moving and traveling in these three-year intervals. And go to the more expensive states like Hawaii, and places like Germany, Alaska, Panama, and Korea. I don't know if Matt has been completely happy with all of his jobs. I do know that some of the places he was just as ready to leave as I was. We've really gone through some changes during this tour.

Matt has come across some real winners here! Yes I am trying to be nice about it. Because you know that's really not what I wanted to say. The army just isn't at all what it used to be. When Matt and I first entered army living we saw a lot of togetherness and family.

People seemed to care about each other. People helped each other out and some of Matt's Superiors seemed to be trying to take him under their wings and teach him the ways of the military and help him to become a better officer. Lately the military has gone in a different direction it seems. Nowadays people don't try to help you.

Everyday I keep asking Matt, "have you called branch yet to see what our options are for our next duty station?" You always want to get a jump on where you might be headed, so you can get some information on the place. I like to find out about the schools, housing, the job market, the crime rate and things of that nature. It's always good to find out things so you won't be too lost in the new city. I always like to call ahead and get housing packets and maybe talk to real estate agents, especially if on-post housing has a waiting list.

I like to find out about the neighborhoods. You never can be too safe. Matt and I hoped that we would get somewhere close to our hometown. We were pretty tired of being so far away from family. It made it difficult especially when Matt went to the field or on deployments.

I had noone to help me or any family around for support. I know our families would have loved to share in the younger years of Matt Jr. and spoil him rotten. Career changes. This is what I am dreading the most. Uck! Another job hunt.

I am however, considering going back to school. I just feel like there is something out there that I should be doing but I just can't grasp it yet. I have so many mixed emotions that I honestly just don't know sometimes. Because we move so much it is hard to grasp your career goals. I have goals; it's just taking me a little longer to reach them than I anticipated.

CHAPTER FIVE

Matthew and I experienced trauma this past Christmas. Around October of 1993 I found out that I was pregnant. Matt was happy because he wanted a little girl. Not to say that this baby would have been a little girl, but we were hopeful. And ladies we all know what starts to go through our minds now.

Lord, we are definitely going to need a three or four bedroom house. Oh the gloom and despair of mid morning feedings and dirty diapers. Ewe! Did I really want to start this all over again? Matt Jr. was only three years old.

Could I handle two toddlers at the same time? Oh man I would be crazy! Or I would drive Matt crazy, one or the other! So I was suffering between a little excitement and a little fear. More fear than excitement I think.

I started feeling tired and ill early on. I am anemic so I figured that was where those feelings were coming from. Usually the symptoms from my anemia would subside after a few days but the feelings were not going away. I knew something just was not right. I drove myself to Tripler Army Medical Center and told the doctor I was not feeling well and had been experiencing a little bleeding.

He proceeded to give me a pelvic exam and I started bleeding like a running faucet. The doctor called for the nurse and a bedpan. I panicked. I told the nurse to call Matt. I was scared. The next thing I knew they were putting me on a rolling bed and wheeling me up to emergency.

I was having a miscarriage. This was 2 ½ weeks before Christmas. The tears just would not stop rolling down my cheeks. I tried and tried not to cry but I wasn't strong enough. When I woke up in recovery Matt was there.

I had such a nauseating feeling and I don't know if it was from the anesthesia or from grief. I know that Matt was just as sad as I was but I think he was trying to be strong for me. Yes I was all to pieces! I suffer from Fibroid disease so I didn't know if this was the cause or not. Doctors say that it happens.

But you still wonder what you could have or should have done differently. Whether you did something wrong. You search your soul trying to figure out why. For months after this I had several bad days. More crying, more bad days.

Do you ever get over loosing a baby? I don't think so. The people in Matthew's unit were very kind. They sent flowers and rendered support to him. As time draws near for us to leave Hawaii, I just sit and wonder what the next place will be like.

Military people, they just wait for their next assignments. Because even though you might choose to go somewhere, that doesn't mean that's where you'll be sent. I know that sounds terrible but after a while you get use to it. And you learn to adjust. Me, I just expect the worst and become totally shocked if it is actually tolerable. Nowadays the military post isn't even as safe as you would think.

On the news you hear about so many killings that actually happen on post, it's scary. Although things like this happen in the cities all the time, you tend to feel a little more secure on post or at least at one time or another you did. But now I really don't know. No matter where we live I always keep my doors locked and pray for my families safety. And Matt and I have gotten so use to living off post that I don't know if we will live on post again.

Although in actuality it might not be, to me it feels like you have just a little bit more privacy off post than you do on post. And you feel like you have to share everything. They tell you that you can't do wallpaper and they don't want you putting large holes in the walls to hang items. You just have to be so particular with the things that you do.

Well, it's August and Matt just left on a TDY trip to Kansas for school. I'm sure he'll be fine but I just wish I could be there with him. Our son Matthew isn't taking this trip very well. He really misses his dad. Every day he asks where is daddy, and he'll say, "I need my daddy."

It is so depressing. It seems that the older he gets the more he understands and the harder it is. But he talks to his dad on the phone so that makes it a little better. Trauma strikes when you least expect it. Things happen that are beyond your control.

In July I was at work when I received a phone call from my sister. My grandmother whom I had lived with my whole life had suffered a massive heart attack. She collapsed at home and was taken to the hospital in Tarboro, North Carolina. This was so very hard for me. I was trying to secure a plane ticket to get home and Matt was planning his change of command ceremony.

This was so stressful. I couldn't ask him to go to the funeral but I was a nervous wreck. I wanted to be there for him during his change of command ceremony but I had to go home. All I could think about was getting there to see her. What if she didn't make it?

What if I didn't make it there to see her? Matt was very supportive. I know he wanted to be there for me. I had not seen her since I moved to Hawaii. When I got to the airport my aunt and uncle were there to pick me up.

I didn't make it. She died before I got there. I was choking back the tears all the way from the airport to her house. My family told me that she hung on as long as she could. And when they told her that I was on my way there to see her, she quietly died.

I struggled for a moment trying to get myself together because

I had not seen any of my family in over two and a half years. I did not want to fall apart in front of my mother. I wanted to be strong for her and my sister. Could I pull this off? I don't know if I can. I can't.

As soon as I saw my mother I wanted to fall apart. I didn't. I greeted all of my family and then made a dash to the restroom where I engaged in a hysterical but quiet nervous breakdown. I had been with my grandmother forever or so it seemed. Thank God I left Matt Jr. with his dad.

These times would not have been good for him. I called Matt to let him know my flight was good and I was there safely. I told him that she did not make it. He was sad. Matt had a relationship with my grandmother also.

He put Matt Jr. on the phone. Talking to my baby made me feel just a little better. Oh how I wanted this to be over. This is not what I wanted my first visit back home to be for. The day of the funeral was another bad day.

One of the worse possible days I have encountered. Ok, I have to figure out a way to make it through this day. Several times I felt nauseous but I managed to get through it. A few times I felt like I was hyperventilating and needed to breath in a paper bag or something. I thought to myself if I was feeling this bad; I could only imagine how her daughters were taking it.

My mother and my aunts that is. They all seem to be ok on the outside but I know that on the inside they were in just as much pain as I was. What will we do without her? She was sweet and took care of everyone. All the young kids were at her house all the time.

All the adults gathered there for Sunday dinner. The funeral was tough. I barely made it through without passing out. I had to leave out a few times. It was really hard seeing her lying there lifeless. She was always a vibrant whippersnapper keeping everyone in check.

She didn't take any mess from anyone. She would read you in a minute and let you know what she wanted you to know; not holding back at all. After the funeral I flew back to Hawaii. My two Matt's were at the airport waiting for me to arrive.

I was glad to be back home but still a little sad. I'm going to miss my grandmother. She was special to all of us. Well it is almost time for a new duty station, a new town, a new beginning and the cycle continues. Where to now? Somewhere lousy or somewhere great.

We just have to wait and see. After my grandmother passed we were thinking that hopefully we could get a duty station close to home. We both had attended Elizabeth City State University. That is where we met. They had an ROTC program there and at some of the surrounding cities in Virginia.

CHAPTER SIX

Well Matt was lucky enough to get an assignment as a Professor of Military Science at ECSU. Elizabeth City was about one hour from Matt's family and about one hour and forty minutes from my family. We were excited about it. A little ready to go. We definitely will miss Hawaii.

I mean who wouldn't miss Hawaii. It was the Aloha State. Beautiful is what it was. A tad bit expensive but the weather was great. We definitely will miss it but we were darn sure ready to leave.

Elizabeth City, North Carolina. A small town. Yep, small town is what it is. No big malls, no Outback Steakhouse, no Red Lobster, no Olive Garden, No Hechts, and no Dillard's. Oh my God! Yes we were off to good old Elizabeth City.

Matt had gotten that assignment as a Professor of Military Science at the University. When we left Hawaii we went to visit our families before we ventured off to Elizabeth City. The visit was nice. We were so tired from the flight that we slept for a day. Matt Jr was so cranky and tired also.

We really didn't get to visit for a couple of days. It took us that long to rest up. But we were glad to see our families. After the visit we headed to Elizabeth City. Matt had to check in with the Commander and then we went house hunting.

Not that again. Yes I was saying the same thing. Here we go again. How many houses have I lived in? I lost count because there were so many.

And now I am getting ready to add another one to the list. Well it had been a really long time since we had been here so we were trying to familiarize ourselves with the town again. We really hadn't been back since we graduated. I had been back for a couple of homecoming events but that was it. I had several friends that lived here that I always kept in touch with, but I had forgotten a lot of things about the town.

We remembered some of the main spots like the mall and the college, and the hospital, things like that. We were trying to find housing developments that were nice. I always thought about Matt Jr. and I being at home alone sometimes when Matthew had to travel or go TDY or on field assignments so I wanted to feel safe. That was one of the main factors that we considered when house hunting. So we searched and we searched for several days until we found a few prospects.

We checked them out and finally chose one. It was not too far from the university where Matthew would be working. It was a nice area near the United States Coast Guard Base. Once again; the wait for household goods. Once we found a house we had to schedule our household goods to be delivered.

I was so glad to get our things. But the worse was yet to come. You know it has taken me this long but I have finally noticed something. That every time we get settled into a new house and we get our household goods in Matthew is on his way to his new job and I am stuck unpacking all of those darn boxes! See, moving has given me memory loss!

And so the unpacking begins. What will be missing this time? Lord only knows. But I was really breaking my neck to find a box with something very special to me in it. When I was living in Hawaii I had a set of trunks hand carved and made for me.

They were beautiful and I fell in love with them. I would have hunted down every moving company worker that had touched my things like a bear smelling fresh fish if those trunks had been missing. (hee hee). First box, no not in there, second box no not in there, ok I am getting a little ansie now. Hum! Oh, I found them. Ok now the world can rest easy because if I hadn't found those trunks I would definitely have had to make a 911 call.

It would definitely take me a few days to unpack but I was a pro at this now. I had figured out how to move it out one room at a time. I was on a roll. I had to make my way to the bedroom because that was the most important room. A good nights sleep after moving.

Yep…Yep…Yep…Yep…a good night's sleep was mandatory. Of course Matt Jr. was certain that the toy box should have been the first one unpacked. He was looking at me like I had lost my mind. I could read those little eyes. They were saying, " Hey lady are ya crazy!

Locate the toy box first. Oh and the frig, make sure that there is cereal and milk around." He could care less about the furniture. He was just looking for the toys. Just the toys.

But like I said, I was not a rookie at this. No military wife is. You know I had a backpack with toys in it and a reserve zip lock bag of cereal. And of course one of the first stops we made before we went to the house was the store to get some milk.

I am not crazy. If I did not have cereal and milk I would have had to send that boy to work with his dad. Because there was no way I was going to risk being alone with him without firepower! He had always been an active little man and very well mannered but there were just some things that you did not mess with when it came to him. Cereal and Milk were some of them.

Emergency backpack full of toys was another. I carried that backpack like a purse. Just stick a little money in the corner and keep a rolling. Yes all the military wives that are reading this are rolling in their seats with laughter and probably any mother out there is laughing as well. Those are the rules.

It's either be stocked with firepower or suffer a nervous breakdown, one or the other. I would take the firepower any day wouldn't you! After a few days I had the whole house unpacked and ready to go. I don't like boxes lying around. I would just as well get it over with so that we can be comfortable.

Meanwhile Matthew was adjusting to his new job. This was going to be a really different assignment. He would be working with college cadets during this assignment. A new challenge. So what surprises will come with this one.

Please God, this military life has aged my heart twenty years already. I hope this one will be smooth sailing. Matthew felt he was going to be ok because some of the people that were there when we were in school were still here. And to repeat those magic words again. It's job-hunting time.

Oh not again! Maybe I'll just do the housewife thing. No, I don't know if I could handle that, well maybe I would consider it. Decisions Decisions. Don't you just hate them!

I dread this moment with a passion. Pavement pounding, interviews, classified, what a rut. Ladies are you with me! I could really kick up like a baby and whine and cry, "I don't wanna look for a job, don't make me." (hee hee hee). And I can just see Matthew looking at me like I must have fallen off the turnip truck and bumped my head acting like that.

Yeah I just hadn't kicked that shopping habit yet so I've got to get a job! But maybe I'll take a week or two to mope around about it. Yes that sounds good to me. Army wives, are you with me! In the meantime I started looking for a daycare for Matt Jr.

I needed to acquire a daycare before I started the job hunt anyway, because that was an all day thing. There were a few around so I started the hunt. Matt also asked some of his co-workers at the university for some recommendations. They had a few also. So I chose one and got Matt Jr. registered in and then the dreadful job hunt began.

Yippee! Yeah right! Who was I fooling? I was miserable. Army wives am I right or wrong. Every time we have to do this it feels like we have to start all the way at the very bottom of the barrel and work our way back up to the top.

Most people look at your resume and see that every three or four years you change jobs. Even though your explanation is that my spouse is military, that doesn't make your chances any better. More so they make your chances worse because people don't want to spend the money training you only to know that in a few years you will be leaving. It really sucks. But ladies that's how it is for us right?

I was hoping that since I was no stranger to the city I would be able to find a job right away but that was not the case. Frustration kicked in and that feeling of wanting to give up was huge. Why did I have to go through this again? Ok Val, maybe you should play with the thought of giving up shopping. Just giving it up.

Ok was I thinking straight or had I completely lost my mind! Yeah I think I have completely lost my mind. How could I even consider giving up shopping? Which was more torture, job-hunting, giving up shopping, job hunting, giving up shopping. My head hurts now.

Was giving up shopping even an option for a woman? Ok this must really be getting to me. I am talking to myself. I think I might have answered back a couple of times. Oh boy. I think I need to lie down.

I feel faint! I started daydreaming about shoes and scarves to match. Could I throw in the towel? Heck no! Why did I even ponder the thought? Absolutely crazy is what I was.

I tell you this job hunting will make anyone crazy. Ok I think that I am ok now. So I pull out the classifieds and start to search. Everyday same thing, search search. At least Matt Jr. was really enjoying his new daycare.

The people there were exceptionally nice and very good with the children. They gave the kids one on one attention. He was happy when I dropped him off and happy when I picked him up. Of course there was a teacher there that kind of took Matt Jr. under her wing and really spoiled him rotten. He learned a lot with her.

Meanwhile my search was not going so well. After a month or so I found a temporary position as an administrative assistant. It was a start. I wasn't too happy with the temporary part of it but I was working. That was the important part.

Of course I wasn't going to stop my job hunt because as I said the job that I got was a temporary hire. I was looking for something permanent. After a few days I got to meet some of Matthew's cadets. They were very nice students. Most of them seemed excited about ROTC.

Although Matthew had never worked in this kind of capacity before I thought he would make a great teacher. If it were something that he was passionate about he would do very well at it. The cadets took to him right off. He brought excitement to the program. He motivated them.

He was a hard hat for the physical training program. He could have been a spokesperson for the "Be All That You Can Be" army commercial. He was very physically fit even though he had injured his back during his military career. He was motivated when it came to the PT program. He tried to keep the cadets motivated also. He wanted them to be in the best shape possible.

I never forget, he would come home sometimes and talk about the crazy cadences they would sing while running during their pt sessions in the early mornings. And as early as they had to get up to do pt in the mornings, they definitely needed some major motivation. I know I would be dragging having to get up that time of the morning and do a full circle of exercise training. It wasn't just a few push-ups and that's all. They did a full workout.

It wasn't long before Matthew settled right in with the ROTC program. He was really getting to know the cadets and was having a great time working with all of them. Before long they all were like an extended family. We had them over for dinner quite often. They also took to Matt Jr. as well.

He enjoyed the cadets as much as we did. I had really gotten good at cooking by then. I was your regular Kee Kee Crocker. (that's a cool name for a good cook) The cadets were not going to turn down a home cooked meal. Especially since most of them did not go home very often.

They either lived too far away or they were just too busy with school and the program to go home. So Matt and I welcomed them all into our home whenever they wanted to stop by. It was nothing for me to come home from work and bake an apple pie or make a pound cake. I enjoyed it. I did not enjoy the pounds that it was putting on me though.

I could have really done without that part of it. But as I said earlier, Matt insisted on home cooked meals. I mean full course ones. Fried pork chops with mashed potatoes and gravy, biscuits, corn on the cob and apple pie a la mode. Doesn't that just scream weight gain!

The messed up part about it was he exercised everyday with the cadets. Matt jr. was always active in daycare and he loved to play outside after school. Me on the other hand hated exercising with a passion! Push-ups, sit-ups yuck! No way I was exercising.

So I could not eat those full course meals everyday like he and the cadets did. That was a bummer. Do you know how difficult it is to cook a full course meal like that and not eat it? Unless you have will power like wonder woman it ain't happening! I did not have Wonder Woman will power!

Ok, I was loosing my younger days of the sleek body. It just was not happening anymore. Don't you just hate that? You keep looking in the mirror like the weight is going to jump up and run and you are going to be skinny again! Fat chance. It ain't happening I tell you!

And on the brighter side of things in the mist of all of this one of my neighbors came over one day and told me about a job that she knew of. I checked it out and went out to apply. It was a local area job which was good. I did not want to commute to Virginia. Remember, I hated driving.

It was a really good job with excellent benefits and I had my fingers crossed that I would get it. I waited and what do you know. I got a call a few days later with a job offer. I accepted the job. Wow! This was great.

I could not wait to start my new job. This was a step up for me. Not at the very bottom of the barrel. Look out, my shopping was back on! There is a God!

I was a little nervous as usual when starting a new job. There weren't a lot of women working there but I didn't mind that. This was a good new beginning. All of them weren't like that. Sometimes new beginnings were so bad it would make you sick.

Homecoming events at the area university were coming up. We hadn't attended one in years. I had actually forgotten how crowded they usually were. The ROTC program was going to be in the parade so Matthew had a few late afternoons working on the float. The parade was always on Saturday mornings.

It was crowded. I took Matt Jr. Too many people. Just too many people for me. But I knew Matt Jr. would enjoy it. So I suffered through the crowds.

Then there was the football game and a few other events like a step show, a concert, an alumni dance. I didn't know if I could handle all of the events. The crowd was killing me. I went to the game. Too many people. I did however see a few people that I had attended college with.

That was a nice surprise. But I am not a big football fan so I didn't watch a lot of the game. Later that evening we went to the step show. That is an event where the fraternities and sororities do skits and step dances competitively. It is really neat.

By the time the step show was over I was beat. I was so ready to go home and kick off my shoes I did not know what to do. There was no way I would make it to the other events. Maybe next year. It was fun though.

Halloween was coming up and Matthew and his cadets came up with a brilliant idea to host a haunted house as a fundraiser at the university. They had all sorts of ideas they were dreaming up. They were drawing up plans and borrowing gadgets, the works. They started building the props and making costumes. They were also printing up flyers and posting around town.

We heard about other groups possibly having haunted houses during Halloween so Matt and the cadets were not sure how theirs was going to turn out. But they continued to work hard at it getting it ready for Halloween. Matt Jr. went out to the university a few times with his dad to help with the haunted house. He was just as excited. He couldn't wait.

The haunted house was held for three nights. It was a real hit. I went out for a little while just to see how it was going. I wasn't crazy enough to go through the haunted house though. I am a scardy cat so I was not ready for a heart attack.

While I was there I heard people running through screaming at the top of their lungs and running. Oh my God! I knew there was no way I was going through it then. I heard all sorts of noises. I heard a chain saw and some kind of creaking noise like a coffin opening and closing.

No way Jose'! Some of the people that came out of there were still shaking and screaming when they got to the end. And even though they were scared out of their minds, some of them turned right around and went back through again and again. I know. I am laughing hysterically too!

The ROTC haunted house was a big hit. Matthew and the cadets and the other staff did really well with the fundraiser. People were talking about it weeks after it was over. They were sure they would do it again the next year. They all had a great time working with it.

This duty station was a little different from the others. We were not on a base so we were not surrounded by the military. Even though I worked on the Coast Guard base here in Elizabeth City it still was not the same. There were bases located in Virginia that we visited sometimes but as I said before it was a little different this time. Was I missing it?

There wasn't the wives group, or coffees to attend. But there were military support all around us. In the summer the program held a military ball. That was a function for the program where the cadets had a formal dinner dance and they chose a Mr. And Mrs. ROTC. Yes, ladies it was an opportunity to acquire a new dress, shoes and a purse. Not that we need any excuse to get a new outfit, but if one were to arise, we would not let it go to waste!

CHAPTER SEVEN

We were actually enjoying living in Elizabeth City. It was a great place to raise a child and it is not crowded and hectic. I would have loved to have a bigger mall but I could adjust. So we decided to buy a house. This was a major decision.

Did we really want to make this step? We had never considered buying a home before because we never stayed in one place long enough. We could have purchased a home at some of those places but then we would have to sell when we got ready to pcs to another duty station or rent it out and worry about keeping it up. So we chose not too. We felt that was the best thing to do.

So we were thinking about it now. Does that mean we are ready to give up this military life? That was a question for Matthew. I don't know if he was sure about this or not. I know he was not sure about leaving the military. It had provided us with a very good life for many years.

So we went on the hunt to find a house in a good neighborhood and close to both of our jobs. We had decided that we would try to be here for a little longer than the other duty stations; maybe Matthew would even retire here. We drove around to a couple of neighborhoods looking at houses for sale. We saw a few that we liked. We weren't sure if we wanted a one story or a two story.

I had always dreamed about owning a two-story house. I don't know why because who wants to clean a big house. We finally found a single story ranch house in a nice quite neighborhood and so we purchased it. I was excited about our new house. But I was not excited about moving again.

Yes, I know, I should be use to it by now, but I don't think you ever get use to moving. You just do it. And the cycle continues. If you haven't figured it out by now military life is like an adventure. The adventure is all in what you make of it.

So to all of the military spouses out their, I applaud you. We are strong and we should be recognized. Why? Because, I lived an Army Life, I was an Army Wife.

✦ THE END ✦